梁燕 编著

炒 馔

Stir-fry

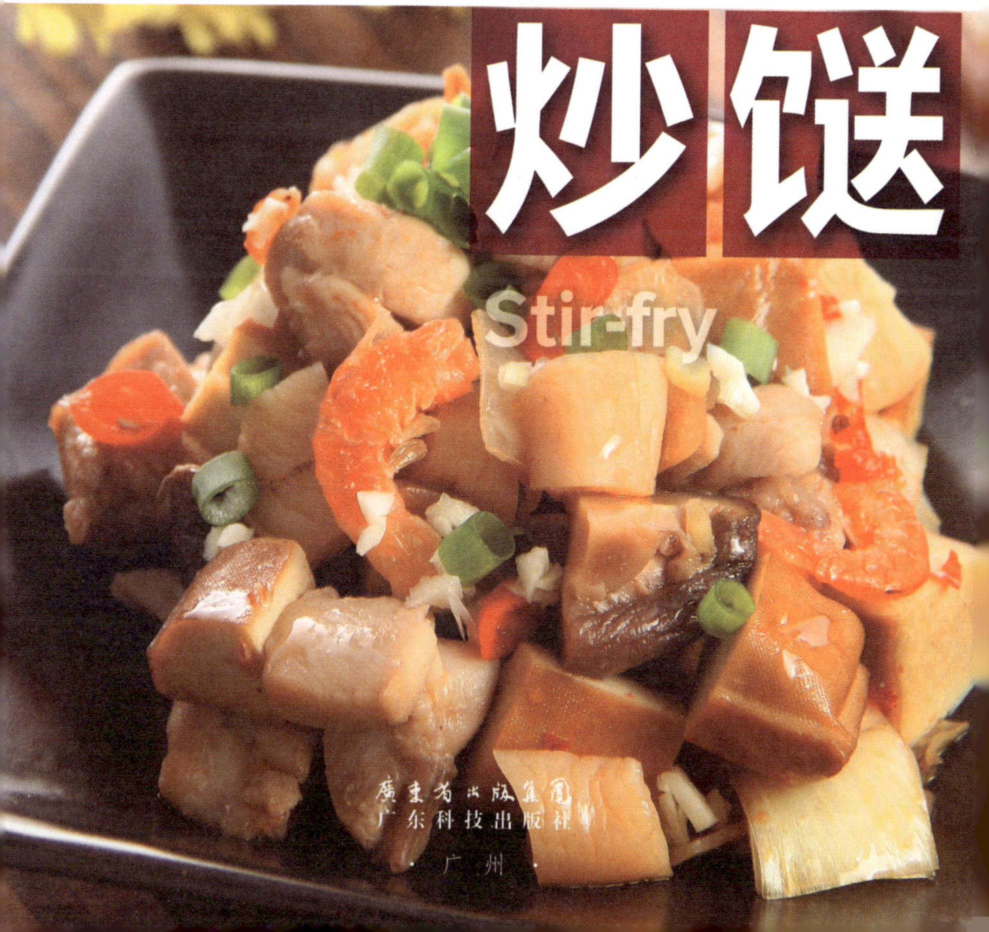

广东为出版集团
广东科技出版社
· 广 州 ·

图书在版编目(CIP)数据

炒馇/梁燕编著.—广州:广东科技出版社,2012.8
(鲜香惹味广东菜)
ISBN 978-7-5359-5719-1

Ⅰ.①炒… Ⅱ.①梁… Ⅲ.①粤菜—炒菜—菜谱
Ⅳ.① TS972.182.65

中国版本图书馆CIP数据核字(2012)第131253号

本书中文简体版由香港万里机构出版有限公司授权广东科技出版社在中国内地出版发行。
广东省版权局著作权合同登记
图字:19-2012-044号

责任编辑:刘 耕　赵雅雅　姚 芸
责任校对:罗美玲
责任印制:罗华之　何小红
出版发行:广东科技出版社
　　　　(广州市环市东路水荫路11号　邮政编码:510075)
　　　　E-mail: gdkjzbb@21cn.com
　　　　http://www.gdstp.com.cn
经　销:广东新华发行集团股份有限公司
印　刷:东莞市翔盈印务有限公司
　　　　(东莞市东城区莞龙路柏洲边路段　邮政编码:523113)
规　格:889mm×1 194mm　1/32　印张3　字数70千
版　次:2012年8月第1版
　　　　2012年8月第1次印刷
定　价:12.00元

如发现因印装质量问题影响阅读,请与承印厂联系调换。

忙人、懒人、达人 的 健康美食攻略

面对大都市快节奏、高压力的生活现状，我们推出了这套《鲜香惹味广东菜》，以**省时、省事、省心、好味、营养**为特色，倡导简约、时尚、健康的饮食理念。书中囊括了广东菜最常见的蒸、炒、煲、炆、煮、炖等烹饪方法，以一日三餐的居家菜为主，强调以味为先，清而不淡，浓而不腻，注重时令，健康为尚。

书中所选食谱均为简单易学，又精致地道的广东特色菜。除了有材料、调料和做法的详细介绍，还包括食材的选购和基本处理方法、常用技巧等技术要点；同时提供每款菜的烹饪时间、人数参考等信息。中英文对照的呈现形式，给即将到国外留学、远离家乡的朋友们提供了不错的参考。"美食达人心动试味"及"Tips"栏目的居家烹饪心得，细致、周到又贴心。

《鲜香惹味广东菜》为都市里的**忙人、懒人、达人**精心设计了一套全面的健康美食攻略，解决您舌尖上的种种疑问，达成您舌尖上的美好愿望。

目录 Contents

看图买材料 Buy ingredients according to the pictures	1
买回来的材料怎么处理？What to do with the ingredients?	5
买回来的材料怎样储存？How to deal with the ingredients bought？	7
炒饪也好味 Stir-fry	7

开始炒饪 Start Stir-frying

🦐 水产 Aquatic

XO酱炒虾仁 Stir-fried shrimps with XO sauce	9
虾仁炒滑蛋 Scrambled eggs with shrimps	11
韭菜沙葛炒蚬米 Stir-fried mini clams with leeks and shage	13
沙拉虾仁 Fried shrimps in salad dressing	15
淮盐虾 Salt and pepper shrimps	17
姜葱炒蟹 Stir-fried crabs with ginger and spring onion	19
胡椒炒蟹 Stir-fried crabs with pepper	21
胜瓜雪耳炒生鱼片 Stir-fried snakehead with angled luffa and ear fungus	23
豉椒炒鲜鱿 Stir-fried squid in black bean sauce	25
时蔬炒鱼块 Stir-fried fish fillets with vegetables	27
咸酸菜炒鱼松 Stir-fried fish slices with pickled cabbage	29
珊瑚蚌炒蜜糖豆 Stir-fried canadian red sea cucumber meat with sweet pea pods	31
象拔蚌炒西兰花 Geoduck clam with broccoli	33

🐔 家禽 Poultry

菠萝鸡片 Stir-fried chicken with pickled pineapple	35
洋葱炒鸭片 Stir-fried onion with duck pieces	37
酱爆鸡球 Stir-fried chicken pieces in bean paste	39
腰果炒鸡丁 Stir-fried dice chicken with cashew nuts	41
蜜味柚子炒鸡球 Stir-fried chicken in pummelo honey sauce	43
五彩杂锦丁 Stir-fried colorful assorted dice	45
三丝炒烟鸭胸 Stir-fried smoked duck breast with vegetable shreds	47

張勳良
2017年购于美国

| 乾隆炒鸽松 Stir-fried pigeon meat | 49 |

猪牛 Pork and Beef

菜心炒牛肉 Fried beef with Choi Sum	51
菠萝炒牛柳 Saute beef tenderloin with pineapple	53
豉汁凉瓜炒牛肉 Stir-fried beef with bitter gourd in fermented black beans sauce	55
香蒜牛肉粒 Stir-fried beef dice with garlic	57
荷豆炒腊肠 Stir-fried Chinese sausage with snow pea pods	59
面筋肉碎炒芹菜 Stir-fried Chinese celery with deep-fried beanburd balls and minced pork	61
回锅肉 Double-cooked pork	63

蔬菜 Vegetables

炒素杂锦 Stir-fried assorted vegetables	65
酱爆四季豆 Saute green beans with bean paste	67
炒杂菜 Stir-fried mixed vegetables	69
番茄炒蛋 Scrambled eggs with tomatoes	71
蒜蓉椒丝炒生菜 Stir-fried lettuce with chopped garlic and red chilli shreds	73
雪菜炒年糕 Stir-fried pudding cake with snow cabbage	75
惹味酱炒通菜 Stir-fried water spinach with flavored paste	77
素翅炒蛋白 Stir-fried artificial shark fin with egg whites	79
素菜竹荪扒菜胆 Stir-fried vegetables with bamboo fungus	81

烹饪小词典 Cooking key words

常用调味品 Common seasonings	84
做菜和味道的常用语 Common phrases of cooking and tastes	88
常用技巧 Common skills	89
一餐中各种食物的摄取比例 The proportion of different food intake during a meal	90
看颜色食果蔬 Choose vegetables and fruit according to colour	91

看图买材料
Buy ingredients according to the pictures

牛肉（炒）：要带少许肥肉。
beef (for frying): Should contains a little fat.

猪肉（炒）：要购买梅柳肉，梅柳肉比较腍。
pork (for frying): Purchase Mei Liu as the texture is more tender.

鱼柳：颜色鲜明。
fillets: Bright colors.

蚬：蚬壳开了不合的，即表示死了，不可购买。
clam: Should not buy clams with shell opens as that means the clam is dead.

鲜蟹：拍拍蟹盖，蟹的眼睛活动得很灵活表示未死
fresh crab: Pat the shells of the crabs, the crab is alive if the eyes are very flexible.

鲜虾：有光泽，虾头不要呈黑色
shrimp: Shrimps should look shiny. Do not buy those with black heads.

生鱼：身上没有瘀红或伤痕。
raw fish: Do not have any red or stasis wound.

蜜糖豆：要青绿而脆。
honey pea pods: Green and crispy.

番茄：红色、圆、大。
tomatoes: Round, big and red in color.

洋葱：完整光滑，没有损伤。
onion: Complete and smooth and not rotten.

沙葛：表面没有损伤。
shage: Surface is not rotten.

韭黄：要黄色，尾部不要变黑和烂。
chives: Yellow in color, the tail part should not be black and rotten.

年糕：颜色要白，不要有黑点。
pudding cake: Color should be white and do not have black spots.

咸酸菜：不要选择太黄的，可能加了色素。
pickled cabbage: Do not choose those in dark yellow color, a pigment may be added.

酸姜：浸着酸姜的醋要清澈。
pickled ginger: The vinegar soaking the ginger should be clear.

XO酱：成分要多瑶柱。
XO sauce: Should contains more dried scallops.

买回来的材料怎么处理？
What to do with the ingredients?

㓥蟹 Gut Crabs

洗蟹：用牙刷刷去脚边的污泥，但要小心扎着的绳不要松脱。

Clean crabs: Brush the feet of crabs with a toothbrush but not to loose the rope holding the crabs.

㓥蟹步骤见下图：

See the pictures below for cutting crabs:

切牛肉 Cut Beef

牛肉顺着横纹切才不会韧。
Cut beef with against the stripes to avoid the tough texture.

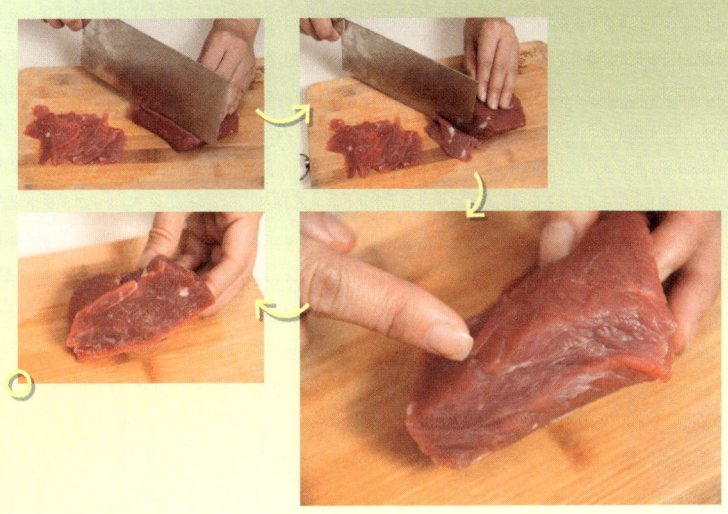

切鱼片 Cut Fish Fillets

鱼肉切第一刀时不要切断，要余下少许，再切第二刀就要切断，两片鱼肉都要薄。
Do not cut off the fish at first knife to leave a little, then cut off at the second knife, two slices should be thin.

买回来的材料怎样储存？
How to deal with the ingredients bought？

鱼：买回来要即时放入冰箱保持新鲜。
Fish: Put the fish into the refrigerator immediately after buying to keep fresh.
虾：去壳去肠，洗净，用少许盐水浸泡，放入冰箱，可令虾爽脆。
Shrimp: Shell and devein shrimp, rinse and soak with some salty water. Put in refrigerator can keep the texture crispy.
菜：买回来要保持新鲜，用纸包好，放入冰箱。
Vegetables: To maintain vegetables fresh, wrapped in newspapper and place in the refrigerator.
辣椒：放冰箱内可保存数个月。
Pepper: Peppers can be stored in the fridge for a few months.

炒餸也好味
Stir-fry

原理：以油作为传热媒介，将加工好的食材用旺火快速加热，充分搅拌，使油、食材和调味料迅速融合而成菜。

Principle: Oil is the heat transfer medium: heat the processed ingredients over high heat quickly, stir-fry thoroughly to integrate oil, ingredients and seasonings into a dish.

优点：保持食材的鲜味；调味方法变化多，味觉和视觉上丰富多彩。

Advantages: To maintain the freshness of ingredients. Variety in seasonings, taste and visual effect is rich.

开始炒餸
Start Stir-frying

Aquatic

美食达人心动试味 / Gourmet's Comments

青红椒要快炒,不要炒太久才会爽脆和颜色鲜艳。

When stir-frying green and red peppers, do not fry for too long to keep the texture crisp and colors bright.

Stir-fried shrimps with XO sauce
XO酱炒虾仁

⏱ 20 分钟 / Minutes 👥 4 人 / Persons

Tips

虾洗净后放水龙头下冲水15分钟,用厨房纸抹干水分才加腌料,再放冰箱中冷藏1小时,可令虾肉爽脆。

Place shrimps under running tap for 15 minutes. Wipe dry with kitchen paper before adding the marinade, and put in the fridge for 1 hour to make the shrimps crispy.

材料	中虾250克 / 青灯笼椒1只 / 红灯笼椒1只 / 蒜头3瓣 料酒适量
腌料	胡椒粉1/2茶匙 / 盐1/2茶匙 / 鸡蛋白1/2只
汁料	蚝油2茶匙 / XO酱1茶匙 / 糖1/2茶匙 / 麻油1/2茶匙

Ingredients	250 g medium prawns / 1 green bell pepper / 1 red bell pepper / 3 cloves garlic / wine
Marinade	1/2 tsp pepper / 1/2 tsp salt / 1/2 egg white
Sauce	2 tsps oyster sauce / 1 tsp XO sauce / 1/2 tsp sugar / 1/2 tsp sesame oil

做法 Method

1. Shell and devein shrimps, rinse, cut at the back, add marinade and mix well.
2. Peel garlic, rinse and chop finely.
3. Rinse green and red bell peppers, seed and cut into irregular shapes.
4. Heat wok with oil about 1/2 tbsp, saute garlic, add green and red bell peppers and stir well. Then add sauce and drizzle wine, stir-fry until shrimps done. Serve.

1. 虾去壳去肠，洗净，在背后剪开，加入腌料拌匀。
2. 蒜头去衣，洗净剁蓉。
3. 青、红灯笼椒洗净，去籽，切滚刀块。
4. 将锅烧热，下油约1/2汤匙，爆香蒜蓉，下青、红灯笼椒炒匀，再加入汁料，潲酒，下虾仁炒全熟即可上碟。

水产 / Aquatic

美食达人心动试味 / Gourmet's Comments

炒好的虾仁炒蛋不要出水,鸡蛋要炒得嫩滑需要多加些油。

Scrambled eggs with shrimps should not have excess water, add some oil when stir-frying eggs to make the eggs tender.

Scrambled eggs with shrimps
虾仁炒滑蛋

⏱ **15** 分钟 / Minutes 👥 **4** 人 / Persons

Tips

将鸡蛋打匀后加入少许生粉,可以令虾仁炒蛋不会出水。

Add some cornstarch when beating the eggs could prevent the scrambled eggs from excessing water.

材料	虾仁220克 / 鸡蛋6只
腌料	盐1/2茶匙 / 胡椒粉1/2茶匙 / 鸡蛋白1/2只 / 生粉1/2茶匙
调味料	盐1/2茶匙 / 生粉少许

Ingredients	220 g shrimp / 6 eggs
Marinade	1/2 tsp salt / 1/2 tsp pepper / 1/2 egg white / 1/2 tsp cornstarch
Seasoning	1/2 tsp salt / cornstarch

Method

1. Devein shrimps, clean and wipe dry, add marinade and mix well.
2. Heat the wok, add 1 tbsp of oil, stir-fry shrimps until 80% done, dish up and let cool.
3. Put eggs into a large bowl, mix into egg mixture.
4. Add shrimps into the beaten egg, add seasonings and mix well.
5. Heat the wok, add 1 tbsp of oil, pour into the egg mixture with shrimps, quickly stir-fry until egg solidifies, dish up.

做法

1. 虾仁去肠,洗净后抹干水分,加入腌料略腌。
2. 将锅烧热,下油约1汤匙,用大火炒虾仁至八成熟,盛起待凉。
3. 将鸡蛋打入大碗中,拌匀成蛋液。
4. 将虾仁放入打好的蛋液中,加入调味料拌匀。
5. 将锅烧热,下油约1汤匙,将虾仁蛋液倒入,快速炒至蛋液凝固,盛起。

水产 Aquatic

美食达人心动试味 / Gourmet's Comments
蚬米经油爆香,整碟馔更香口。
Saute dried mini clams in oil could make the whole dish more tasty.

Stir-fried mini clams with leeks and shage
韭菜沙葛炒蚬米

⏱ 25 分钟 Minutes 👥 4 人 Persons

Tips
沙葛有季节性,如买不到可改用豆腐干或马蹄。
Shage is a seasonal ingredient, it could be replaced by beancurd or water chestnuts.

材料 沙葛1/2个 / 韭菜200克 / 蚬米150克 / 蒜蓉1汤匙
调味料 盐1/2茶匙 / 胡椒粉1/2茶匙 / 糖1/3茶匙

Ingredients 1/2 shage / 200 g leek / 150 g mini clams / 1 tbsp chopped garlic
Seasoning 1/2 tsp salt / 1/2 tsp pepper / 1/3 tsp sugar

做法 Method

1. Rinse leek, cut the old stems and section.
2. Peel shage, rinse and cut into strips.
3. Rinse mini clams and drain.
4. Heat wok with 1/2 tbsp of oil, saute chopped garlic. Stir-fry shage and mini clams, add seasonings and some water, mix well, cover and cook for a while.
5. Finally, add leek and stir well.

1. 韭菜洗净，去老梗，切段。
2. 沙葛去皮，洗净切条。
3. 蚬米洗净，沥干水分。
4. 将锅烧热，下油约1/2汤匙，爆香蒜蓉，加入沙葛和蚬米略炒，下调味料和少许水拌匀，加盖稍焗片刻。
5. 最后加入韭菜略炒匀即可。

Aquatic

美食达人心动试味 / Gourmet's Comments

沙拉配虾味道很好，但不可太早加沙拉酱，否则会"出水"。

Salad with shrimps tastes good, but do not add salad dressing too early or water will comes out.

Fried shrimps in salad dressing
沙拉虾仁

25 Minutes · 4 Persons

Tips

炒好虾后，可以不加沙拉酱，待上碟才挤上沙拉酱。

Add salad dressing after dishing up the shrimps but nor right after deep-frying the shrimps.

材料	中虾400克 / 青椒1个 / 沙拉酱2汤匙 / 面粉2茶匙
腌料	鸡蛋白1只 / 生粉1.5茶匙 / 胡椒粉1/2茶匙 / 盐1/4茶匙

Ingredients	400 g prawns / 1 green pepper / 2 tbsps salad dressing / 2 tsps flour
Marinade	1 egg white / 1.5 tsps cornstarch / 1/2 tsp pepper / 1/4 tsp salt

做法 Method

1. Shell shrimps, cut open the back to the gut and remove the intestine, rinse and drain. Marinate for 10 minutes.
2. Rinse green peppers, cut in halves, seed and cut into irregular pieces.
3. Put flour onto a plate, pounce shrimps with flour.
4. Heat the wok, add a bowl of oil. When oil is boiling, deep-fry the shrimps until done. Remove and absorb the oil by kitchen paper.
5. Heat the wok again, add 1/2 tbsp of oil, green pepper and shrimp back to wok, mix well. Finally add a little salad dressing and stir well. serve.

1. 中虾去壳，背部剖开去肠，洗净，沥干水分，以腌料腌10分钟。
2. 青椒洗净，切半，去籽，切滚刀块。
3. 面粉放碟中，将中虾扑上面粉。
4. 将锅烧热，下油约1碗，待油烧滚后下中虾炸至熟，取出并用厨房纸稍吸去油分。
5. 再将锅烧热，下油约1/2汤匙，将青椒和虾回锅拌匀，最后加入沙拉酱少许炒匀上碟。

Aquatic

美食达人心动试味 / Gourmet's Comments

淮盐要撒得适中和平均,加上葱花更增添香味,葱不可缺。
The amount of salt and pepper should be moderate and average, spring onion is indispensable as it adds more flavor.

Salt and pepper shrimps
淮盐虾

⏱ 30 分钟 / Minutes   👥 4 人 / Persons

Tips

淮盐可以自己做:以白锅炒香盐和五香粉即成淮盐。
Peeper salt can be DIY, stir-fry salt and pepper until fragrant.

材料 中虾450克 / 红辣椒1只 / 蒜蓉3汤匙 / 葱花2汤匙 / 姜蓉2茶匙

腌料 生粉2茶匙 / 鸡粉1茶匙 / 盐1/2茶匙

调味料 准盐1/2茶匙

Ingredients	450 g prawns / 1 red chilli / 3 tbsps chopped garlic / 2 tbsps chopped spring onion / 2 tsps chopped ginger
Marinade	2 tsps cornstarch / 1 tsp chicken powder / 1/2 tsp salt
Seasoning	1/2 tsp spiced salt

做法

1. Shell shrimps, cut open the back to the gut and remove, rinse and drain. Marinate for 10 minutes.
2. Rinse red chilli, seed and chop.
3. Put flour onto a plate, pounce shrimps with flour.
4. Heat the wok, add 1 tbsp of oil until oil boiling, fry the shrimps until golden.
5. Heat the wok again, add 1/2 tbsp of oil, saute chopped garlic, chilli and ginger. Put the shrimps back to the wok, add seasoning and mix well, sprinkle chopped spring onion. Serve.

1. 中虾去壳,背部剖开去肠,洗净,沥干水分,以腌料腌10分钟。
2. 辣椒洗净,去籽,切碎。
3. 面粉放碟中,将中虾扑上面粉。
4. 将锅烧热,下油约1汤匙,待油烧滚后下中虾煎至金黄盛起。
5. 再将锅烧热,下油约1/2汤匙,爆香蒜蓉、辣椒蓉和姜蓉,将中虾回锅,下调味料拌匀,撒下葱花即可上碟。

Aquatic

美食达人心动试味 | *Gourmet's Comments*

姜和葱的分量要比较多,才会更惹味。
The amount of ginger and spring onion should be abundant to make the dish more tasty.

Stir-fried crabs with ginger and spring onion
姜葱炒蟹

⏱ 30 分钟 / Minutes   👥 4 人 / Persons

Tips

肉蟹扑上生粉才走油,可锁住蟹的肉汁。
Gravy of the crabs could be reserved when they are pounced with cornstarch before blanching in oil.

| 材料 | 肉蟹2只 / 姜10片 / 葱10棵 / 蒜头5瓣 / 生粉2汤匙 / 米酒2茶匙 |
| 调味料 | 胡椒粉1茶匙 / 盐1/2茶匙 / 糖1/3茶匙 |

| Ingredients | 2 crabs / 10 slices ginger / 10 stalks spring onion / 5 cloves garlic / 2 tbsps cornstarch / 2 tsps rice wine |
| Seasoning | 1 tsp pepper / 1/2 tsp salt / 1/3 tsp sugar |

做法 / Method

1. Gut crabs, rinse and cut into pieces and drain.
2. Rinse spring onion, cut the roots and tails, cut into sections.
3. Put cornstarch onto a plate, pounce crabs with cornstarch
4. Heat wok, add cup of oil until boiling, add crabs and cook until 70% done. Remove and absorb excess oil by kitchen paper.
5. Heat the wok again, 1/2 tbsp of oil, saute ginger slices and spring onion sections. Return crabs to the wok, add seasonings, drizzle wine, mix well and dish up.

1. 肉蟹㓥好，洗净切件，沥干水分。
2. 葱洗净，切去根部和尾部，切段。
3. 生粉放碟中，将肉蟹扑上生粉。
4. 将锅烧热，下油约1碗，待油烧滚后下肉蟹走油至7成熟，取出并用厨房纸稍吸去油分。
5. 再将锅烧热，下油约1/2汤匙，爆香姜片和葱段，将蟹回锅，加调味料，潜酒，拌匀即可上碟。

Aquatic

美食达人心动试味 / Gourmet's Comments
要炒得干身,令胡椒沾满整只蟹。
The body of crabs should be dry and covered with whole pepper.

Stir-fried crabs with pepper
胡椒炒蟹

⏱ 30 分钟 / Minutes　👥 4 人 / Persons

Tips
白锅炒香胡椒粒,将其中1/3压碎,味道会比较浓郁。
Saute pepper in wok without adding oil, then crush 1/3 of the pepper, the taste would be rich.

材料	肉蟹2只 / 姜片120克 / 葱段100克 / 葱头4粒 / 蒜头4瓣 / 辣椒3只 / 鲜胡椒50克 / 米酒2茶匙
腌料	鱼露1/2茶匙
调味料	糖1茶匙 / 盐1/2茶匙

Ingredients 2 crabs / 120 g ginger slices / 100 g spring onion sections / 4 cloves shallot / 4 cloves garlic / 3 red chilli / 50 g fresh pepper / 2 tsps rice wine

Marinade 1/2 tsp fish sauce

Seasoning 1 tsp sugar / 1/2 tsp salt

做法 / Method

1. Gut crabs, rinse and cut into pieces, drain, marinate for 10 minutes.
2. Rinse shallots and garlic, peel and pat with a chopper. Rinse red chilli, seed and chop.
3. Put cornstarch onto a plate, pounce crabs with cornstarch.
4. Heat wok, add cup of oil until boiling, add crabs and cook until 50% done. Remove and absorb excess oil by kitchen paper.
5. Heat the wok again, add 1/2 tbsp of oil, saute ginger, spring onion, shallots, garlic, chili and fresh pepper, return crabs back to the wok, stir-fry until aroma comes out. Drizzle wine, add seasonings and mix well, cover the wok and cook for 5 minutes.
6. Add spring onion sections and mix well. Serve.

1. 肉蟹刣好，洗净切件，沥干水分，加入腌料腌10分钟。
2. 葱头、蒜头洗净，去衣，用刀略拍。辣椒洗净，去籽，切碎。
3. 面粉放碟中，将肉蟹扑上生粉。
4. 将锅烧热，下油约1碗，待油烧滚后下肉蟹走油至5成熟，取出并用厨房纸稍吸去油分。
5. 再将锅烧热，下油约1/2汤匙，爆香姜片、葱段、葱头、蒜头、辣椒和鲜胡椒，将肉蟹回锅，炒至香味溢出，潵酒，加入调味料拌匀，盖上锅盖焗5分钟。
6. 加葱段拌匀即可上碟。

Aquatic

美食达人心动试味 | *Gourmet's Comments*

炒鱼片要轻轻炒，不要将鱼肉炒碎。
Stir-fry snakehaed gently to avoid breaking it into pieces.

Stir-fried snakehead with angled luffa and ear fungus
胜瓜雪耳炒生鱼片

⏱ 20 分钟 / Minutes   👥 4 人 / Persons

Tips

1 雪耳可用木耳代替，木耳有通血管的效用。
Ear fungus can be replaced by black fungus, black fungus has positive vascular effects.

2 生鱼可请鱼档代为去骨起肉。
May ask the staff to help to remove the bone of snakehead.

材料　　胜瓜（丝瓜）2条 / 雪耳4朵 / 生鱼（去骨）1条 / 蒜蓉2茶匙
　　　　姜2片
腌料　　盐1/4茶匙 / 胡椒粉少许
调味料　盐1/2茶匙 / 鸡粉1/2茶匙 / 生抽1/2茶匙 / 糖1/4茶匙 / 水1/2杯

Ingredients　2 angled luffas / 4 ear fungus / 1 snakehead fish (boneless)
　　　　　　2 tsps chopped garlic / 2 slices ginger
Marinade　　1/4 tsp salt / pepper
Seasoning　 1/2 tsp salt / 1/2 tsp chicken powder / 1/2 tsp light soy sauce
　　　　　　1/4 tsp sugar / 1/2 cup water

做法 Method

1. Peel angled luffa, rinse and cut into irregular pieces.
2. Soak ear fungus until soft, rinse and remove stalks, cut into small pieces.
3. Rinse snakehead, butterfly, marinate and mix well.
4. Heat wok with 1/2 tbsp of oil, saute chopped garlic and ginger slices, add angled luffa and ear fungus and stir-fry until done, add seasonings and mix well.
5. Add snakehead slices and gently stir-fry until done.

1. 胜瓜去皮，洗净，切滚刀块。
2. 雪耳浸发后洗净，去蒂，切小朵。
3. 生鱼洗净，切双飞片，下腌料拌匀。
4. 将锅烧热，下油约1/2汤匙，爆香蒜蓉和姜片，下胜瓜和雪耳炒至熟，加入调味料拌匀。
5. 加入生鱼片，轻轻炒至熟透即可。

水产 Aquatic

美食达人心动试味 / Gourmet's Comments

鲜鱿不要炒太久,否则会太韧。
Do not stir-fry squid for too long or it will become too tough.

Stir-fried squid in black bean sauce
豉椒炒鲜鱿

⏱ 25 分钟 / Minutes   👥 4 人 / Persons

Tips

鲜鱿鱼要在鱿鱼的肚内一面划花刀,划十字时,刀和鲜鱿鱼要呈45°斜角,先横划,再直划。

Cut checkers pattern on the belly side of the squid. The chppoer should be in 45 degree angle with the squid, cut horizontally first and then vertically.

| 材料 | 鲜鱿鱼500克 / 西芹100克 / 蒜蓉2茶匙 / 干葱4粒 / 青椒1只 / 红灯笼椒1只 / 豆豉1汤匙 / 米酒2茶匙 |
| 芡汁 | 蚝油2茶匙 / 麻油1/2茶匙 / 生粉1/2茶匙 / 糖1/4茶匙 / 水4汤匙 |

| Ingredients | 500 g fresh squid / 100 g celery / 2 tsps chopped garlic / 4 cloves shallot / 1 green pepper / 1 red bell pepper / 1 tbsp fermented black beans / 2 tsps rice wine |
| Sauce | 2 tsps oyster sauce / 1/2 tsp sesame oil / 1/2 tsp cornstarch / 1/4 tsp sugar / 4 tbsps water |

做法 / Method

1. Rinse fresh squid, remove the membrane and internal organs. Cut checkers pattern on the surface of the squid.
2. Rinse celery and torn the woody fibers away.
3. Rinse green pepper and red bell pepper, seed and cut into pieces. Rinse shallots, peel and pat with a chopper.
4. Crush fermented black beans briefly, put into a bowl, add some water and mix well.
5. Heat the wok with 1/2 tbsp of oil, saute chopped garlic, shallots, fermented black beans, add squid and stir well. Drizzle wine, add celery, green peppers, red bell peppers and sauce and stir well. Serve.

1. 鲜鱿鱼洗净，撕去薄膜和除去内脏，划花刀。
2. 西芹洗净，撕去老筋。
3. 青椒和红灯笼椒洗净，去籽，切件。干葱洗净，去衣，用刀略拍。
4. 豆豉略为压蓉，放碗中，加少许水开匀。
5. 将锅烧热，下油约1/2汤匙，爆香蒜蓉、干葱、豆豉，加入鲜鱿炒匀，溅酒，炒片刻即加入西芹、青椒、红灯笼椒和芡汁炒匀即可上碟。

 水产 Aquatic

美食达人心动试味 / Gourmet's Comments

鱼没有腥味。炒好的菜心要青绿,但不要太生。

Marinate fish with wine could remove the unpleasant smell. Cooked vegetables should be green in color but not too raw.

Stir-fried fish fillets with vegetables
时蔬炒鱼块

⏱ 20 分钟 / Minutes   👥 4 人 / Persons

Tips

鱼柳加酒腌可除去鱼的腥味。

Marinate fish fillets with wine can remove the unpleasant smell.

材料　菜心200克／鱼柳2条／姜2片／米酒2茶匙
腌料　鸡蛋白1/2只／酒1茶匙／生粉1茶匙／胡椒粉1/2茶匙
　　　鸡粉1/2茶匙
调味料　盐1/2茶匙／糖1/3茶匙

Ingredients　200 g Choi Sum / 2 slices fish fillet / 2 slices ginger
2 tsps rice wine
Marinade　1/2 egg white / 1 tsp wine / 1 tsp cornstarch / 1/2 tsp pepper
1/2 tsp chicken powder
Seasoning　1/2 tsp salt / 1/3 tsp sugar

做法

1. Rinse fish fillets, cut into pieces, drain, marinate for about 15 minutes.
2. Discard old leaves of Choi Sum, rinse and cut into sections.
3. Heat the wok, add a bowl of oil until boiling, add fish fillets and cook until 70% done, remove and absorb excess oil by kitchen paper.
4. Heat the wok again, add 1/2 tbsp of oil, saute ginger slices, saute Choi Sum, add seasonings and mix well, return fish fillets to wok, stir well, drizzle wine. Serve.

1. 鱼柳洗净，切成鱼块，沥干水分，加入腌料拌匀，腌约15分钟。
2. 菜心弃掉老叶，洗净，切段。
3. 将锅烧热，下油约1碗，待油烧滚后下鱼块走油至7成熟，取出并用厨房纸稍吸去油分。
4. 再将锅烧热，下油约1/2汤匙，爆香姜片，下菜心略炒，加调味料拌匀，将鱼块回锅炒匀，瀳酒即可上碟。

Aquatic

美食达人心动试味 / Gourmet's Comments

咸酸菜不可炒太久,要爽口。
Pickled cabbage should not be stir-fried for too long to reseve the crispy texture.

Stir-fried fish slices with pickled cabbage
咸酸菜炒鱼松

⏱ 20 分钟 / Minutes   👥 4 人 / Persons

Tips

咸酸菜用盐水略浸可减去咸味。
The salty taste of pickled cabbage could be reduced if soaked in salty water.

材料	咸酸菜梗2块 / 原味鲮鱼肉馅200克 / 红灯笼椒1只 / 蒜蓉1茶匙 / 葱2棵（切段）
腌料	胡椒粉1/2茶匙 / 盐1/2茶匙 / 生粉1.5茶匙 / 水2汤匙
调味料	生粉1茶匙 / 生抽2茶匙 / 糖2茶匙 / 麻油1/2茶匙 / 胡椒粉1/2茶匙

Ingredients	2 stems pickled cabbage / 200 g minced dace (original flavor) / 1 red bell pepper / 1 tsp chopped garlic / 2 stalks spring onion (sectioned)
Marinade	1/2 tsp pepper / 1/2 tsp salt / 1.5 tsps cornstarch / 2 tbsps water
Seasoning	1 tsp cornstarch / 2 tsps light soy sauce / 2 tsps sugar / 1/2 tsp sesame oil / 1/2 tsp pepper

做法

1. Rinse pickled cabbage stems, shredd, soak in salty water for 15 minutes, drain and squeeze out excess water.
2. Marinate minced dace for 15 minutes.
3. Rinse red bell pepper, seed and shred.
4. Heat wok, add 1/2 tbsp of oil, fry minced dace, presse into a round pie, fry until golden on both sides, let cool and cut into strips.
5. Heat the wok with 1/2 tbsp of oil, saute chopped garlic, red bell pepper, pickled cabbage stems and stripped minced dace. Add seasoning and spring onion and mix well.

1. 咸酸菜梗洗净，切丝，用加了盐的水浸15分钟，挤干水分待用。
2. 鲮鱼肉馅加腌料腌15分钟。
3. 红灯笼椒洗净，去籽，切丝。
4. 将锅烧热，下油约1/2汤匙，下鲮鱼肉馅，压成圆饼形，煎至两面金黄，待凉后切成条状。
5. 将锅烧热，下油约1/2汤匙，爆香蒜蓉，下红灯笼椒、咸酸菜，鲮鱼肉条，加入调味料和葱段拌匀即可。

水产 Aquatic

美食达人心动试味 / Gourmet's Comments

蜜糖豆不要炒得太腍。
The sweet pea pods don't be overcooked.

Stir-fried canadian red sea cucumber meat with sweet pea pods
珊瑚蚌炒蜜糖豆

⏱ 25 分钟 Minutes   👥 4 人 Persons

Tips

蜜糖豆要飞水去除草青味。
Blanch sweet pea pods to remove the grass flavor.

材料	珊瑚蚌180克 / 蜜糖豆150克 / 芹菜2棵 / 中虾8只 / 干葱蓉2茶匙 / 姜末1茶匙 / 米酒2茶匙
腌料	胡椒粉2茶匙 / 生粉1/2茶匙 / 鸡粉1/4茶匙
芡汁	蚝油1.5汤匙 / 生粉2茶匙 / 麻油1/2茶匙 / 鸡粉1/2茶匙 / 水3汤匙

Ingredients	180 g Canadian red sea cucumber meat / 150 g sweet pea pods / 2 stalks Chinese celery / 8 medium shrimps / 2 tsps chopped shallot / 1 tsp minced ginger / 2 tsps rice wine
Marinade	2 tsps pepper / 1/2 tsp cornstarch / 1/4 tsp chicken powder
Sauce	1.5 tbsps oyster sauce / 2 tsps cornstarch / 1/2 tsp sesame oil / 1/2 tsp chicken powder / 3 tbsps water

做法 / Method

1. Rinse Canadian red sea cucumber meat, drain for later use.
2. Rinse the sweet pea pods, remove the woody outer fibers on both sides, blanch.
3. Rinse Chinese celery, cut the roots and leaves, section.
4. Rinse the shrimps, shell and devein, rinse under the tap for 10 minutes and drain. Add marinade and mix well, put in the refrigerator for 30 minutes.
5. Heat the wok with 1/2 tbsp of oil, saute minced ginger and shallots, add the shrimps and Canadian red sea cucumber meat, drizzle wine, stir-fry until aroma comes out.
6. Mix the sauce in a bowl, cook until boils, add sweet pea pods and Chinese celery, stir-fry until sauce is slightly dried. Serve.

1. 珊瑚蚌洗净，沥干水分备用。
2. 蜜糖豆洗净，摘去两边老筋，飞水备用。
3. 芹菜洗净，切去根部和叶，切段。
4. 中虾洗净，去壳去肠，放水龙头下冲10分钟，沥干水分。加腌料拌匀，放冰箱中半小时。
5. 将锅烧热，下油约1/2汤匙，爆香姜末和干葱蓉，加入中虾和珊瑚蚌略炒，潶酒，炒至香味溢出。
6. 芡汁放碗中拌匀，下芡汁煮滚，再放蜜糖豆和芹菜，炒至芡汁稍收干即可上碟。

美食达人心动试味 / Gourmet's Comments

西兰花飞水时不要煮得太腍。
Blanch broccoli to remove the grass flavor, do not overcook.

Geoduck clam with broccoli
象拔蚌炒西兰花

⏱ 15 分钟 / Minutes　　👥 6 人 / Persons

Tips

这款菜用了快炒方法,简单方便又容易处理,但是必须谨记即炒即吃。
This frying method is simple and easy to handle but remember that the dishes must be served hot.

材料	西兰花1个（约250克） / 象拔蚌200克 / 蒜蓉1茶匙 姜汁1茶匙
芡汁	清鸡汤3汤匙 / 生抽2茶匙 / 生粉1茶匙 / 糖1/2茶匙 麻油少许

Ingredients	1 pc broccoli (around 250g) / 200 g geoduck clam 1 tsp chopped garlic / 1 tsp ginger sauce
Sauce	3 tbsps chicken broth / 2 tsps light soy sauce 1 tsp caltrop starch 1/2 tsp sugar / a pinch of sesame oil

做法

1. Cut geoduck clam into thin slices.
2. Wash broccoli and cut into small pieces.
3. Heat a wok of water, add 1 tbsp of oil, parboil broccoli and drain.
4. Heat 2 tbsps of oil, saut garlic, toss with geoduck clam quickly, stir in ginger sauce and broccoli, then toss with sauce until well combined and dish up.

1. 象拔蚌切薄片。

2. 西兰花洗净，切细。

3. 烧热1锅水，下1汤匙油，放入西兰花飞水，沥干。

4. 烧热2汤匙油，爆香蒜蓉，下象拔蚌快手兜炒，再加入姜汁和西兰花，下芡汁炒匀便可上碟。

美食达人心动试味 / Gourmet's Comments

菠萝只要拌炒数下就可以，不可炒太久，否则会令鸡肉变霉（不新鲜、无弹性）。

Do not stir-fry pineapple for too long, otherwise the chicken will lose freshness and stretch.

Stir-fried chicken with pickled pineapple
菠萝鸡片

🕐 25 分钟 / Minutes　　👥 4 人 / Persons

Tips

菠萝可以用新鲜的，但调味的糖要多加一些。

Fresh pineapple can be used but some more sugar is needed.

材料	罐头菠萝1罐（235克）/ 鸡腿1只 / 蒜头4瓣 / 葱3棵（切段）/ 子姜160克
腌料	生粉1茶匙 / 盐1/2茶匙 / 胡椒粉1/2茶匙 / 糖1/3茶匙
调味料	生抽1/2茶匙 / 麻油1/2茶匙 / 糖1/4茶匙 / 生粉1/2茶匙 / 水1汤匙

Ingredients	1 can canned pineapple (235 g) / 1 chicken thigh / 4 cloves garlic / 3 stalks spring onion(sectioned) / 160 g young ginger
Marinade	1 tsp cornstarch / 1/2 tsp salt / 1/2 tsp pepper / 1/3 tsp sugar
Seasoning	1/2 tsp light soy sauce / 1/2 tsp sesame oil / 1/4 tsp sugar / 1/2 tsp cornstarch / 1 tbsp water

做法

1. Rinse chicken thigh, remove bone, slice, marinate for 30 minutes.
2. Cut pineapple into pieces, retaine 1/2 cup of syrup.
3. Heat wok with 1/2 tbsp of oil, saute garlic, stir-fry chicken pieces until done.
4. Cook syrup for a moment, add seasonings, young ginger and spring onion and mix well, add pineapple and stir well. Serve.

1. 鸡腿洗净，去骨，切片，以腌料腌30分钟。
2. 菠萝切件，糖水1/2杯留用。
3. 将锅烧热，下油约1/2汤匙，爆香蒜头，下鸡片炒至熟。
4. 将糖水加入煮片刻，加入调味料、子姜和葱段拌匀，下菠萝炒匀即可。

美食达人心动试味 / Gourmet's Comments

洋葱炒至刚软身就可以了。
Stir-fry onion until just soft but not too long.

Stir-fried onion with duck pieces
洋葱炒鸭片

⏱ 35 分钟 Minutes 👥 4 人 Persons

Tips

鸭尾有膻味，如果用整只鸭，不要忘记除去鸭尾的鸭子（鸭屁股）。
Remember to remove the white piece in duck tail, or there will be the smell of mutton.

材料	鸭胸肉2大块／洋葱1个／蒜蓉1汤匙／葱3棵／姜末1茶匙 米酒2茶匙
腌料	生粉1茶匙／盐1/2茶匙／生抽1/2茶匙／胡椒粉1/2茶匙
调味料	老抽1/2茶匙／生抽1/2茶匙／糖1/3茶匙／生粉水1汤匙

Ingredients	2 large pieces duck breast / 1 onion / 1 tbsp chopped garlic 3 stalks spring onion / 1 tsp minced ginger / 2 tsps rice wine
Marinade	1 tsp cornstarch / 1/2 tsp salt / 1/2 tsp light soy sauce / 1/2 tsp pepper
Seasoning	1/2 tsp dark soy sauce / 1/2 tsp light soy sauce / 1/3 tsp sugar 1 tbsp cornstarch solution

做法

1. Rinse duck breast, slice, marinate for 30 minutes.
2. Peel onions, rinse and shred.
3. Rinse spring onion, rinse and cut into sections.
4. Heat wok with 1/2 tbsp of oil, saute onion, add some salt and stir-fry until slightly brown, dish up.
5. Heat the wok again, add 1/2 tbsp of oil, saute chopped garlic and ginger, stir-fry duck pieces until done, return onion to wok, add seasonings and spring onion and mix well, drizzle wine. Serve.

1. 鸭胸肉洗净，切片，下腌料腌30分钟。
2. 洋葱去衣，洗净切丝。
3. 葱洗净，切段。
4. 将锅烧热，下油约1/2汤匙，爆香洋葱，加少许盐炒至微黄色，盛起待用。
5. 再将锅烧热，下油约1/2汤匙，爆香蒜蓉和姜末，下鸭片炒至熟，将洋葱回锅，加入调味料和葱段拌匀，潵酒即可上碟。

Poultry

美食达人心动试味 / Gourmet's Comments

鸡肉不要腌太久,因磨豉酱有咸味,腌久了味道会太咸。
As ground soy paste is salty, the taste will be too salty if the chicken is marinated for a long time

Stir-fried chicken pieces in bean paste
酱爆鸡球

35 分钟 Minutes

3 人 Persons

Tips

每种磨豉酱的咸度不同,所以一定要试味。
Test taste is needed as ground fermented bean paste in different brands are in different salty level.

材料	鸡腿2只 / 干葱头6粒 / 葱6棵 / 姜末2茶匙 / 磨豉酱1汤匙
腌料	酒1汤匙 / 姜汁1茶匙 / 盐1/4茶匙 / 胡椒粉1/4茶匙
调味料	生抽1汤匙 / 糖1茶匙 / 麻油1/2茶匙 / 水1/2杯

Ingredients 2 chicken thigh / 6 cloves shallot / 6 stalks spring onion / 2 tsps minced ginger / 1 tbsp ground soy paste

Marinade 1 tbsp wine / 1 tsp ginger / 1/4 tsp salt / 1/4 tsp pepper

Seasoning 1 tbsp light soy sauce / 1 tsp sugar / 1/2 tsp sesame oil / 1/2 cup water

做法

1. Remove bones from chicken thigh, rinse and cut intp pieces, marinate for 30 minutes.
2. Rinse shallots, peel and pat. Rinse spring onions, Remove roots and tail, cut into sections.
3. Heat wok with 1/2 tbsp of oil, saute shallots, chopped ginger and grounded fermented bean paste, add chicken pieces, spring onion sections and seasoning and stir-fry until done.

1. 鸡腿起肉，洗净，切块，用腌料腌30分钟备用。
2. 干葱洗净，去衣拍扁。葱洗净，切去根部和尾部，切段。
3. 将锅烧热，下油约1/2汤匙，爆香干葱、姜末和磨豉酱，加入鸡块、葱段和调味料炒至鸡肉熟透即可。

Poultry

美食达人心动试味 / Gourmet's Comments

此菜式不要太早煮,要在开饭前才炒,否则腰果会不脆。
Not to cook this dish too early, stir-fried just before dinner, otherise cashew nuts will not be crispy.

Stir-fried dice chicken with cashew nuts
腰果炒鸡丁

⏱ 35 分钟 / Minutes   👥 4 人 / Persons

Tips

腰果要熄火后放入鸡丁中快速拌匀才会脆。
In order to keep the cripsy texture, cashew nuts should be added after turning off the heat.

材料	鸡肉250克 / 腰果100克 / 青椒1个 / 红灯笼椒1个 蒜蓉1茶匙 / 姜末1茶匙
腌料	生粉1茶匙 / 生抽1茶匙 / 盐1/2茶匙 / 鸡粉1/2茶匙
调味料	鱼露1茶匙 / 生抽1茶匙 / 生粉1茶匙 / 水5汤匙

Ingredients	250 g chicken / 100 g cashew nuts / 1 green pepper / 1 red bell pepper / 1 tsp chopped garlic / 1 tsp minced ginger
Marinade	1 tsp cornstarch / 1 tsp light soy sauce / 1/2 tsp salt / 1/2 tsp chicken powder
Seasoning	1 tsp fresh fish sauce / 1 tsp light soy sauce / 1 tsp cornstarch / 5 tbsps water

做法 / Method

1. Rinse cashew nuts, soak in water for 10 minutes and drain. Bake in a preheated oven at 150°C for 20-25 minutes.

2. Rinse chicken and dice, marinate for 20 minutes.

3. Rinse the green pepper and red bell pepper, seed and cut into wedges.

4. Heat wok with 1/2 tbsp of oil, saute chopped garlic and ginger, add chicken add stir-fry until 70% done. Then add green peppers and red bell pepper, fry until the chicken meat done. Add seasoning and mix well, turn off heat, add cashew nuts and mix well. Serve.

1. 腰果洗净，用水浸10分钟后捞起，沥干水分。放入预热至150℃的焗炉内焗20~25分钟。

2. 鸡肉洗净，切丁，加腌料腌20分钟。

3. 青椒和红灯笼椒洗净，去籽，切角。

4. 将锅烧热，下油约1/2汤匙，爆香蒜蓉和姜末，下鸡肉炒至7成熟，再下青椒和红灯笼椒继续炒至鸡肉熟，加调味料拌匀，熄火，下腰果拌匀即可上碟。

Poultry

美食达人心动试味 / Gourmet's Comments

调味料要均匀地沾满鸡球,味道更佳。
It tastes better if chicken is evenly coated with seasoning.

Stir-fried chicken in pummelo honey sauce
蜜味柚子炒鸡球

35 分钟 / Minutes
3 人 / Persons

Tips

鸡肉可改用其他肉类,如牛肉、猪肉或鱼肉。
Chicken meat could be replaced by beef, pork or fish.

材料　鸡腿2只 / 红灯笼椒1个
腌料　蚝油2汤匙 / 生粉2茶匙 / 胡椒粉1/2茶匙
调味料　柚子蜜4汤匙 / 蚝油2茶匙 / 鱼露1/2茶匙 / 生粉1茶匙
　　　　水6汤匙

Ingredients　2 chicken thigh / 1 red bell pepper
Marinade　2 tbsps oyster sauce / 2 tsps cornstarch / 1/2 tsp pepper
Seasoning　4 tbsps pummelo honey / 2 tsps oyster sauce / 1/2 tsp fish sauce
　　　　　 1 tsp cornstarch / 6 tbsps water

做法 Method

1. Remove bones from chicken thigh, rinse and cut into pieces, drain, marinate for 30 minutes.

2. Rinse red bell pepper, seed and cut into shreds.

3. Heat the wok with 1/2 tbsp of oil, fry chicken until golden on both sides, dish up and set aside.

4. Heat wok, add seasonings, bring to a boil, add red pepper shreds and stir-fry, pour onto the chicken. Serve.

1. 鸡腿起肉，洗净，切块，沥干水分，加腌料拌匀，腌30分钟。

2. 红灯笼椒洗净，去籽切丁。

3. 将锅烧热，下油约1/2汤匙，下鸡块煎至两面金黄，盛起备用。

4. 将锅烧热，下调味料，煮滚后加入红灯笼椒丁拌炒匀，淋在鸡块上即可。

Poultry

美食达人心动试味 / Gourmet's Comments

如来不及切丁,可改为切片或切丝,但大小要均匀。
If not have enough time to dice, could slice or shred but still in uniform size.

Stir-fried colorful assorted dice
五彩杂锦丁

25 分钟 Minutes   5 人 Persons

Tips

菜脯可用雪菜代替,其他材料也可随个人口味更改。
Preserved radish could be replaced by pickled vegetables, other ingredients can also be changed according to personal taste.

材料 鸡肉粒150克 / 菜脯粒2汤匙 / 五香豆腐干3件
洋葱粒2汤匙 / 冬菇4只 / 虾米1/4杯 / 红辣椒1只
葱花2汤匙

调味料 豆瓣酱1茶匙 / 蒜蓉2茶匙 / 盐1/4茶匙

Ingredients 150 g chicken dice / 2 tbsps perserved radish dice
3 pieces spiced beancurd / 2 tbsps onion dice / 4 dried black mushrooms
1/4 cup dried shrimps / 1 red chilli / 2 tbsps chopped spring onion

Seasoning 1 tsp chilli bean paste / 2 tsps chopped garlic / 1/4 tsp salt

做法 Method

1. Rinse spiced beancurd and dice.
2. Heat wok with 1/2 tbsp of oil, saute onion, dish up.
3. Heat wok again with 1/2 tbsp of oil, saute dried shrimps, dried black mushrooms, dish up and set aside.
4. Heat wok again with 1/2 tbsp of oil, saute chopped garlic, spring onion dice, chilli bean paste, red chilli, add chicken and stir-fry until 70% done, return other ingredients to wok, stir-fry and mix well. Serve.

1. 五香豆腐干洗净,切粒。
2. 将锅烧热,下油约1/2汤匙,爆香洋葱,盛起备用。
3. 再将锅烧热,下油约1/2汤匙,爆香虾米、冬菇,盛起备用。
4. 再将锅烧热,下油约1/2汤匙,爆香蒜蓉、葱花、豆瓣酱、红辣椒,下鸡肉炒至7成熟,将其他材料回锅,炒匀即可。

家禽 Poultry

美食达人心动试味 / Gourmet's Comments

鸭胸肉切成粒来炒会更甘香。
It tastes better if duck breast is diced.

Stir-fried smoked duck breast with vegetable shreds
三丝炒烟鸭胸

⏱ 20 分钟 / Minutes   👥 4 人 / Persons

Tips

胡萝卜丝要先炒片刻才可加其他材料，因西芹和青椒都比较容易熟。
Stir-fried carrot before adding other Ingredients since celery and green peppers will be cooked in shorter time.

| 材料 | 烟鸭胸1件 / 胡萝卜1/2个 / 西芹2棵 / 青椒1个 / 蒜头2瓣 |
| 调味料 | 生抽1/2茶匙 / 麻油1/2茶匙 / 糖1/3茶匙 / 生粉水1汤匙 |

| Ingredients | 1 piece smoked duck breast / 1/2 carrot / 2 stalks celery / 1 green pepper / 2 cloves garlic |
| Seasoning | 1/2 tsp light soy sauce / 1/2 tsp sesame oil / 1/3 tsp sugar / 1 tbsp cornstarch solution |

做法 Method

1. Peel garlic, cleaning, rinse and pat.
2. Rinse carrot and peel, cut into shreds. Rinse celery, torn away woody fibers, shred. Rinse green peppers, seed and cut into shreds.
3. Heat the wok with 1/2 tbsp of oil, fry smoked duck breast until golden on both sides, dish up.
4. Heat wok with 1/2 tbsp of oil, saute garlic, add carrot shreds, then add celery and green pepper, add seasonings and mix well, return smoked duck breast to wok and mix well. Serve.

1. 蒜头去衣,洗净,拍扁。
2. 胡萝卜洗净,去皮,切丝。西芹洗净,撕去老筋,切丝。青椒洗净,去籽,切丝。
3. 将锅烧热,下油约1/2汤匙,下鸭胸肉煎至两面金黄,待凉切片。
4. 将锅烧热,下油约1/2汤匙,爆香蒜头,下胡萝卜丝略炒,再加入西芹丝和青椒丝,加调味料拌匀,将烟鸭胸回锅拌匀即成。

美食达人心动试味 / Gourmet's Comments

松子仁和腰果一样，不能炒太久。
Just like cashew nuts, pine nuts should not be cooked for too long.

Stir-fried pigeon meat
乾隆炒鸽松

30 分钟 Minutes | 4 人 Persons

Tips

乳鸽可改用蚝豉、瘦肉或鸡肉。
Pigeon can be replaced by dried oysters, lean pork or chicken.

材料	乳鸽1只 / 金华火腿2片 / 冬菇6只 / 胡萝卜1/2根 松子仁2汤匙 / 马蹄12粒 / 生菜1棵 / 葱花1汤匙 蒜蓉1汤匙 / 甜面酱1/2杯 / 米酒2茶匙
腌料	生粉1茶匙 / 盐1/2茶匙 / 胡椒粉1/4茶匙 / 鸡蛋白1只
调味料	糖1茶匙 / 老抽1茶匙 / 米酒1茶匙 / 麻油1/2茶匙 胡椒粉1/4茶匙 / 水1汤匙

Ingredients	1 pigeon / 2 slices Jinhua ham / 6 dried balck mushrooms 1/2 carrot / 2 tbsps pine nuts / 12 water chestnuts / 1 lettuce 1 tbsp chopped spring onion / 1 tbsp chopped garlic 1/2 cup sweet bean paste 2 tsps rice wine
Marinade	1 tsp cornstarch / 1/2 tsp salt / 1/4 tsp pepper / 1 egg white
Seasoning	1 tsp sugar / 1 tsp dark soy sauce / 1 tsp rice wine / 1/2 tsp sesame oil 1/4 tsp pepper / 1 tbsp water

做法 Method

1. Rinse pigeon, remove bones and dice, marinate for 20 minutes.
2. Heat wok, add a bowl of oil until boiling, blanch pigeon, dish up and drain.
3. Rinse water chestnuts and carrot, peel and dice. Rinse lettuce, cut into circles.
4. Rinse dried black mushrooms, soak until sofot. Rinse Jinhua ham, blanch and dice.
5. Heat wok with 1/2 tbsp of oil, saute chopped garlic, add dried black mushrooms, water chestnuts, carrot, Jinhua ham, stir-fry, return pigeon to the wok, drizzle wine, mix well, sprinkle spring onion and pine nut, mix well and dish up.
6. Serve with lettuce and sweet bean paste.

1. 乳鸽洗净，起肉切小块，下腌料腌20分钟。
2. 将锅烧热，下油约1碗，待油烧滚后下乳鸽走油，盛起，沥干油分。
3. 马蹄、胡萝卜洗净，去皮切小块。生菜洗净，修剪成圆形。
4. 冬菇洗净，浸软，去蒂切粒。金华火腿洗净，飞水后切粒。
5. 将锅烧热，下油约1/2汤匙，爆香蒜蓉，加入冬菇、马蹄、胡萝卜、金华火腿粒拌炒，将乳鸽回锅，潵酒，拌匀，撒下葱花、松子仁拌匀，盛起。
6. 吃时用生菜包入馅料，蘸上甜面酱同食。

美食达人心动试味 / Gourmet's Comments

菜心和牛肉是快熟的食材,不用炒太久。
Choi Sum and beef are easily cooked, do not stir-fry for too long.

Fried beef with Choi Sum
菜心炒牛肉

⏱ 25 分钟 / Minutes 👥 3 人 / Persons

Tips

1 牛肉要横纹切。
Cut beef with against the stripes to avoid the tough texture

2 腌牛肉时要先下其他腌料拌匀,再加少量的水,边拌边加,最后加生油盖着。
When marinating beef, add other ingredients and mix well, then gradually add water, mix well, finally add oil to cover the beef.

材料	牛肉150克 / 菜心300克 / 蒜蓉1汤匙
腌料	生抽1茶匙 / 生油1茶匙（后下）/ 糖1/3茶匙 生粉1茶匙 / 水1汤匙
调味料	盐1/2茶匙 / 鸡粉1/2茶匙

Ingredients	150 g beef / 300 g Choi Sum / 1 tbsp chopped garlic
Marinade	1 tsp light soy sauce / 1 tsp oil (addlater) / 1/3 tsp sugar 1 tsp cornstarch / 1 tbsp water
Seasoning	1/2 tsp salt / 1/2 tsp chicken powder

做法

1. Rinse beef and slice, marinate and mix well, cover the surface with oil, leave for 20 minutes.
2. Rinse Choi Sum, cut into sections.
3. Heat wok with 1/2 tbsp of oil, add beef and stir-fry until 70% done.
4. Heat wok again with 1/2 tbsp of oil, saute chopped garlic, Choi Sum and seasonings and stir-fry until 70% done, return beef to wok, stir well and dish up.

1. 牛肉洗净，切片，下腌料拌匀，以油盖面，腌20分钟。
2. 菜心洗净，切段。
3. 将锅烧热，下油约1/2汤匙，下牛肉快手兜匀至7成熟即盛起。
4. 再将锅烧热，下油约1/2汤匙，爆香蒜蓉，下菜心和调味料炒至7成熟，将牛肉回锅，炒匀即可上碟。

美食达人心动试味 / Gourmet's Comments

牛肉烹调时间适中,不会太韧。
Stir-fiy should not be cooked for too long or it will be tough.

Saute beef tenderloin with pineapple
菠萝炒牛柳

10 分钟 / Minutes **4** 人 / Persons

Tips

炒牛肉要以大火快炒。
Beef must be fried over high heat and in short time.

材料	牛柳200克／新鲜菠萝4片／青椒、红椒各1/2个／姜少许／葱1棵
腌料	生抽2茶匙／糖1/2茶匙／生粉1/2茶匙
调味料	茄汁2汤匙／糖1汤匙／生粉1茶匙／水1/3杯

Ingredients	200g beef tenderloin / 4 slices Fresh pineapple / 1/2 green and red bell pepper / ginger / 1 stalk spring onion
Marinade	2 tsps soy sauce / 1/2 tsp sugar / 1/2 tsp cornstarch
Seasoning	2 tbsps ketchup / 1 tbsp sugar / 1 tsp cornstarch / 1/3 cup water

做法

1. Marinate beef tenderloin for 10 minutes. Slice pineapple, dice green and red peppers, section spring onion.
2. Heat wok with 2 tbsp oil, stir-fry beef 80/done, set aside.
3. Hent wok again with 1 tbsp of oil, saute spring onion, ginger, green and red pepper, add pineapple and beef. Thicken with sauce, stir well and serve.

1. 牛柳拌入腌料腌10分钟；菠萝切片；青、红椒切小粒；葱切段。
2. 将锅烧热，下油2汤匙，下牛柳炒至八成熟，取出。
3. 再下1汤匙油，爆香葱、姜、青椒和红椒粒炒片刻，将菠萝、牛柳回锅，埋芡汁炒匀即可。

美食达人心动试味 | **Gourmet's Comments**

凉瓜切较大片会比较爽脆。
Bitter gourd will be more crispy if it is cut in larger pieces.

Stir-fried beef with bitter gourd in termented black beans sauce
豉汁凉瓜炒牛肉

25 分钟 / Minutes　　4 人 / Persons

Tips

凉瓜先用盐腌可令其变软,再洗去盐水,加入少许糖,可令凉瓜减去大部分苦味。

Marinate bitter gourd with salt can make it soft, then rinse away the salt, add some sugar could reduce the bitterness.

材料	牛肉150克 / 凉瓜（苦瓜）2个 / 豆豉1汤匙 / 蒜蓉1汤匙
牛肉腌料	生抽1茶匙 / 生油1茶匙（后下） / 糖1/3茶匙 / 生粉1茶匙 / 水1汤匙
凉瓜腌料	糖2汤匙 / 盐1/2茶匙
调味料	盐1/2茶匙

Ingredients	150 g beef / 2 bitter gourds / 1 tbsp fermented black beans / 1 tbsp chopped garlic
Marinade for Beef	1 tsp light soy sauce / 1 tsp oil (add later) / 1/3 tsp sugar / 1 tsp cornstarch / 1 tbsp water
Marinade for Bitter Gourd	2 tbsps sugar / 1/2 tsp salt
Seasoning	1/2 tsp salt

做法 Method

1. Rinse beef and slice, marinate beef and cover with oil, leave for 20 minutes.
2. Rinse bitter gourd and remove seeds, marinate for 10 minutes.
3. Pat fermented black beans, put in a bowl with a some water, mix well.
4. Heat wok with 1/2 tbsp of oil, add beef and stir-fry until 70% done, dish up.
5. Heat the wok again, add 1/2 tbsp of oil, saute chopped garlic and fermented black beans, then add bitter gourd and season with salt, add water, cook for a while with the lid covered, Return beef to wok. serve.

1. 牛肉洗净，切片，用牛肉腌料拌匀，以油盖面，腌20分钟。
2. 凉瓜洗净，去瓤，切片，加凉瓜腌料腌10分钟。
3. 豆豉压扁，放碗中，用少许水开好备用。
4. 将锅烧热，下油约1/2汤匙，下牛肉快手炒至7成熟即盛起。
5. 再将锅烧热，下油约1/2汤匙，爆香蒜蓉和豆豉，下凉瓜拌炒，加盐调味，加适量水，盖好锅盖煮片刻，将牛肉回锅即可上碟。

Pork and Beef

美食达人心动试味 / Gourmet's Comments

牛肉不会韧。炸蒜蓉一定要后加才不会腍。
Stir-fry beef until only 60%-70% done to keep the soft texture, it will not Ren. Deep-fry garlic should be added later or elase it will become too soft.

Stir-fried beef dice with garlic
香蒜牛肉粒

⏱ 15 分钟 / Minutes   👥 4 人 / Persons

Tips

牛肉只可煎至6~7成熟，才不会太韧。
To keep the soft texture, stir-fry beef until only 60%-70% done.

材料 牛肉500克 / 炸蒜蓉2汤匙 / 蒜头6瓣 / 红辣椒1只
调味料 淮盐1/2茶匙

Ingredients 500 g beef / 2 tbsps deep-fried garlic / 6 cloves garlic / 1 red chilli
Seasoning 1/2 tsp pepper salt

做法 Method

1. Peel garlic, rinse and chop. Rinse red chilli, seed and cut finely.
2. Rinse beef and dice.
3. Heat wok with 1/2 tbsp of oil, turn to medium heat, saute chopped garlic, fry beef until 60% done, add fried garlic and mix well, add red pepper and pepper salt and mix well. Serve.

1. 蒜头去衣，洗净剁蓉。红辣椒洗净，去籽，切小粒。
2. 牛肉洗净，切成方丁。
3. 将锅烧热，下油约1/2汤匙，改用中火，爆香蒜蓉，放入牛肉粒煎至6成熟，加入炸蒜蓉拌匀，加红辣椒粒和淮盐拌匀即可上碟。

Pork and Beef

美食达人心动试味 / Gourmet's Comments

荷兰豆要摘去蒂和筋，否则会有渣。
The roots of snow peas should be removed, or there will be residue.

Stir-fried Chinese sausage with snow pea pods
荷豆炒腊肠

⏱ 15 分钟 / Minutes   👥 4 人 / Persons

Tips

1. 腊肠先要用温水洗去表面的灰尘。
   Chinese sausage should be rinsed in warm water to remove dust on surface.

2. 腊肠蒸熟后，比较容易切片。
   The Chinese sausage could easily sliced after steaming.

材料 腊肠2条 / 荷兰豆120克 / 芹菜50克 / 蒜蓉1/2汤匙 / 姜4片 / 米酒1茶匙

芡汁 上汤3汤匙 / 糖1/3茶匙 / 盐1/3茶匙 / 生粉1茶匙

Ingredients 1 pair of Chinese sausage / 120 g snow pea pods / 50 g Chinese celery / 1/2 tbsp chopped garlic / 4 slices ginger / 1 tsp rice wine

Sauce 3 tbsps soup / 1/3 tsp Sugar / 1/3 tsp salt / 1 tsp cornstarch

做法 Method

1. Rinse Chinese sausage in warm water, remove and put onto a plate.
2. Put a steam rack in the wok, add water to nearly the height of steaming rack, boil water, steam for 10 minutes, let cool and slice.
3. Rinse snow pea pods, torn away the outer woody fibres. Rinse Chinese celery, cut the roots and section.
4. Heat wok with 1/2 tbsp of oil, saute chopped garlic and ginger slices, add snow pea pods and Chinese sausage, add 2 tbsps of water, cover and cook for 1 minute, drizzle wine, add Chinese celery and sauce, stir well. Serve.

1. 腊肠放温水中冲洗，取出置碟中。
2. 在锅中放蒸架，加水至接近蒸架高度，烧滚水，将腊肠用大火隔水蒸约10分钟，取出，待凉后切片。
3. 荷兰豆洗净，撕去老筋。芹菜洗净，切去根部，切段。
4. 将锅烧热，下油约1/2汤匙，爆香蒜蓉和姜片，下荷兰豆和腊肠，加水2汤匙，加盖焗1分钟，溅酒，放芹菜和汁料，炒匀即可上碟。

美食达人心动试味 / Gourmet's Comments

面筋一分为二更容易入味。
Deep-fried beanburd balls absorb more flavor, if they are cut in halves.

Stir-fried Chinese celery with deep-fried beanburd balls and minced pork
面筋肉碎炒芹菜

25 分钟 Minutes   4 人 Persons

Tips

面筋飞水是为了去除生油的味道。
Blanching deep-fried beanburd balls could remove excess oil smell.

材料	面筋6个 / 猪肉馅150克 / 芹菜2棵
腌料	盐1/2茶匙 / 生抽1/2茶匙 / 胡椒粉1/2茶匙
调味料	盐1/2茶匙 / 鸡粉1/2茶匙 / 麻油1/2茶匙

Ingredients	6 deep-fried beanburd balls / 150 g minced pork / 2 stalks Chinese celery
Marinade	1/2 tsp salt / 1/2 tsp light soy sauce / 1/2 tsp pepper
Seasoning	1/2 tsp salt / 1/2 tsp chicken powder / 1/2 tsp sesame oil

做法

1. Marinate minced pork for 20 minutes.
2. Rinse deep-fried beancurd balls and blanch.
3. Rinse Chinese celery, cut woody fibers and remove leaves, rinse and cut into sections.
4. Heat wok with 1/2 tbsp of oil, saute minced pork, stir-fry 70% done, add deep-fried beancurd balls and Chinese celery, add seasoning and mix well.

1. 猪肉馅加腌料腌20分钟。
2. 面筋洗净，飞水。
3. 芹菜洗净，切去根部，去叶，洗净后切段。
4. 将锅烧热，下油约1/2汤匙，爆香绞猪肉，炒至7成熟，加入面筋和芹菜拌匀，下调味料拌匀即可。

美食达人心动试味 / *Gourmet's Comments*

喜欢吃辣的可多加些辣豆瓣酱。
More chilli bean paste could be added according to personal taste.

Double-cooked pork
回锅肉

⏱ 35 分钟 / Minutes 👥 4 人 / Persons

Tips

猪肉要放冰箱冷冻才更易切成薄片。
Chill snow frozen pork in refrigerator before cutting into thin slices.

材料 猪踭肉（猪手上的肉）300克 / 绍菜（大白菜）300克 / 豆腐干3块 / 红灯笼椒1只 / 青椒1只 / 蒜头2瓣

调味料 甜面酱2汤匙 / 辣豆瓣酱2茶匙

汁料 生抽2茶匙 / 盐1/2茶匙 / 糖1/2茶匙 / 老抽1/2茶匙

Ingredients 300 g heel meat of pig / 300 g cabbage / 3 pieces pressed beancurd / 1 red bell pepper / 1 green pepper / 2 cloves garlic

Seasoning 2 tbsps sweet bean paste / 2 tsps chilli bean paste

Sauce 2 tsps light soy sauce / 1/2 tsp salt / 1/2 tsp sugar / 1/2 tsp dark soy sauce

做法 / Method

1. Rinse heel meat of pig. Bring a pot of water to a boil, add heel meat of pig and simmer for 30 minutes over medium heat, pick up and drain, let cool and cut into thin slices.

2. Rinse pressed beancurd and slice. Peel garlic, rinse and slice.

3. Rinse green peppers, red bell pepper, seed, cut into pieces. Rinse cabbage, cut into pieces.

4. Heat wok with 1/2 tbsp of oil, saute green pepper and red bell pepper, dish up.

5. Heat the wok again with 1/2 tbsp of oil saute garlic slices, add green pepper, red bell pepper, pressed beancurd, pork slices and seasoning, stir well, pour the sauce, drizzle wine, add cabbage. Serve.

1. 猪踭肉洗净。烧滚一锅水，下猪踭肉用中火煮30分钟，捞起，沥干水，待凉后切薄片。

2. 豆腐干洗净，切片。蒜头去衣，洗净，切片。

3. 青椒、红灯笼椒洗净，去籽，切块。绍菜洗净，切块。

4. 将锅烧热，下油约1/2汤匙，爆香青椒、红灯笼椒，盛起。

5. 再将锅烧热，下油约1/2汤匙，爆香蒜片，加入青椒、红灯笼椒、豆腐干、猪肉片和调味料炒匀，倒入汁料，溅酒，加入绍菜兜匀后即可上碟。

Vegetables

美食达人心动试味 / Gourmet's Comments

蚝油不要选择太甜的。
Do not choose oyster sauce with sweety favor.

Stir-fried assorted vegetables
炒素杂锦

20 分钟 Minutes 4 Persons 人

Tips

蚝油可改为豆瓣酱,味道较辛辣,可更刺激味蕾。
Oyster sauce could be replaced by chillibean paste in order to have spicy taste.

材料　杂豆4汤匙 / 素鸡1条 / 豆腐干2件 / 胡萝卜1根 / 竹笋1个 / 蒜蓉1汤匙

调味料　蚝油2汤匙 / 糖1茶匙 / 生抽1茶匙 / 盐1/3茶匙

芡汁　生粉1茶匙 / 水2汤匙

Ingredients　4 tbsps assorted beans / 1 vegetarian chicken / 2 pieces pressed beancurd / 1 carrots / 1 bamboo shoots / 1 tbsp chopped garlic

Seasoning　2 tbsps oyster sauce / 1 tsp sugar / 1 light tsp soy sauce / 1/3 tsp salt

Sauce　1 tsp cornstarch / 2 tbsps water

做法 Method

1. Rinse pressed beancurd and vegetarian chicken and dice. Rinse assorted beans and drain.

2. Rinse bamboo shoots, remove woody outer shell, slice and then dice.

3. Heat the wok with 1/2 tbsp of oil, saute chopped garlic, add assorted beans, vegetarian chicken, pressed beancurd and bamboo shoot dice, add seasonings, stir well, thicken with cornstarch solution.

1. 胡萝卜、豆腐干、素鸡洗净，切粒。杂豆洗净，沥干水分。

2. 竹笋洗净，去外壳，切丁。

3. 将锅烧热，下油约1/2汤匙，爆香蒜蓉，加入杂豆、胡萝卜、素鸡、豆腐干和竹笋拌炒，加入调味料炒匀，最后下芡汁勾芡即可。

美食达人心动试味 / Gourmet's Comments

保持了四季豆的翠绿颜色。
Keep the beans green colour.

Saute green beans with bean paste
酱爆四季豆

10 分钟 / Minutes 4 人 / Persons

Tips

注意四季豆的烹调时间不可太长，否则会太脆和变黄。
Don't cook green beans for too long, otherwise they will become too tender and yellowish.

材料　猪肉馅100 克 / 四季豆200 克 / 蒜茸1 茶匙 / 豆瓣酱1 汤匙
调味料　盐1/2 茶匙 / 生抽1/2 茶匙 / 生粉1/2 茶匙 / 糖少许 / 油1 茶匙
芡汁　清鸡汤1/3 杯 / 蚝油1 茶匙 / 生粉1 茶匙 / 糖1/2 茶匙

Ingredients: 100g minced pork / 200g green beans / 1 tsp chopped garlic / 1 tbsp board bean paste

Seasoning: 1/2 tsp salt / 1/2 tsp light soy sauce / 1/2 tsp cornstarch / sugar / 1 tsp oil

Sauce: 1/3 cups chicken broth / 1 tsp oyster sauce / 1 tsp cornstarch / 1/2 tsp sugar

做法 Method

1. Marinate minced pork for 10 minutes. Rinse green beans, cut off edges and remove strings, cut into halves.

2. Boild water, add 1 tbsp oil and blanch the beans. Drain and set aside.

3. Heat wok with 2 tbsp of oil, saute garlic and bean paste, add pork and fry loose. Add sance and boiling, Add green beans, stir-fry over medium heat until the sance dries up. Serve.

1. 猪肉馅加腌料腌10分钟，四季豆洗净，摘去两边老筋，切成两段。

2. 烧开一锅水，下1汤匙油，下四季豆飞水，沥干。

3. 将锅烧热，下2汤匙油，爆香蒜蓉和豆瓣酱，下猪肉馅炒松散，下芡汁煮滚，再放四季豆，以中火炒至芡汁收干即可。

Vegetables

美食达人心动试味 / Gourmet's Comments

芦笋如比较老,要先撕去表面的老衣。
If asparagus is quite old, peel away the surface.

Stir-fried mixed vegetables
炒杂菜

⏱ **20** 分钟 / Minutes 👥 **5** 人 / Persons

Tips

杂菜可转用其他菜,如通菜、菠菜、西兰花等。
Can switch to other mixed vegetable dishes, such as water, spinach, broccoli, spinach and so on.

材料 莲藕1/4个 / 鲜百合2个 / 小芦笋1小扎 / 红辣椒1只（切丝）/ 蒜蓉1汤匙 / 姜丝1茶匙 / 米酒2茶匙

调味料 鱼露2茶匙 / 糖1/2茶匙

Ingredients 1/4 lotus roots / 2 fresh lily bulbs / 1 small bundle asparagus / 1 red chili (shredded) / 1 tbsp chopped garlic / 1 tsp shredded ginger / 2 tsps rice wine

Seasoning 2 tsps fish sauce / 1/2 tsp sugar

做法  Method

1. Peel lotus root, rinse and cut into thin slices.
2. Rinselily lily bulbs, separate.
3. Cut asparagus into sections.
4. Heat wok with 1/2 tbsp of oil, saute chopped garlic, ginger shreds and red chilli, then add lotus root and stir-fry, add asparagus and cook for a while, add lily bulbs. Add seasonings and mix well. Drizzle wine, stir well and dish up.

1. 莲藕去皮，洗净切薄片。
2. 百合洗净，撕成一瓣瓣。
3. 小芦笋洗净，切段。
4. 将锅烧热，下油约1/2汤匙，爆香蒜蓉、姜丝和红辣椒丝，先加入莲藕炒熟，再下小芦笋炒片刻，加入百合和调味料拌匀，潵酒，炒匀即可上碟。

美食达人心动试味 / Gourmet's Comments

番茄最好去皮。
It is better to peel tomatoes.

Scrambled eggs with tomatoes
番茄炒蛋

10 分钟 / Minutes　　4 人 / Persons

Tips

炒番茄不用加水。
Do not add water when stir-frying tomatoes.

| 材料 | 番茄4个 / 鸡蛋4只 / 鱼露2茶匙 |
| 调味料 | 茄汁2汤匙 / 糖1.5茶匙 / 盐1/2茶匙 |

Ingredients 4 tomatoes / 4 eggs / 2 tsps fish sance
Seasoning 2 tbsps ketchup / 1.5 tsp sugar / 1/2 tsp salt

做法 Method

1. Rinse tomatoes, cut into 4 pieces.
2. Beat the eggs in a bowl, add fish sauce and beat into egg mixture.
3. Heat wok with 1/2 tbsp of oil, add tomatoes, add seasonings and stir-fry until cooked but not break, dish up.
4. Heat wok again with tbsp of oil, add eggs, stir-fry until solidifies, add tomatoes done but not breaking, mix well. Serve.

1. 番茄洗净,每个切成4件。
2. 鸡蛋打在碗中,加鱼露打匀成蛋液。
3. 将锅烧热,下油约1/2汤匙,下番茄炒,加调味料炒至番茄腍而不烂,盛起。
4. 再将锅烧热,下油约1汤匙,倒下蛋液,快手炒至凝固,即将番茄回锅,拌匀即可。

美食达人心动试味 / Gourmet's Comments

生菜不可炒太久，否则会变黑和太腍，而且会沾在一起。
Lettuce can not becooked for too long, otherwise it will be black in color and too soft, and will be stick together.

Stir-fried lettuce with chopped garlic and red chilli shreds
蒜蓉椒丝炒生菜

⏱ 10 分钟 / Minutes 👥 4 人 / Persons

Tips

加入红辣椒的馔会比较辣，如不喜欢太辣可不加。
Red chilli should not be added if you do not like spicy dish.

材料 生菜400克 / 蒜蓉2汤匙 / 红辣椒1只
调味料 盐3/4茶匙 / 糖1/2茶匙

Ingredients 400 g lettuce / 2 tbsps chopped garlic / 1 red chilli
Seasoning 3/4 tsp salt / 1/2 tsp sugar

Method

1. Rinse lettuce, cut the roots, cut horizontally into halves or 4 pieces.
2. Rinse red chilli, seed and cut into shreds.
3. Heat the wok with 1/2 tbsp of oil, saute chopped garlic and red chilli, add lettuce and mix well, add seasonings and mix well. Serve.

1. 生菜洗净，切去根部，每棵直切两半或4份备用。
2. 红辣椒洗净，去籽，切丝。
3. 将锅烧热，下油约1/2汤匙，爆香蒜蓉和红辣椒，下生菜炒匀，加入调味料拌匀即可上碟。

蔬菜 Vegetables

美食达人心动试味 / Gourmet's Comments

年糕本身是没有味道的,所以其他材料一定要用足,而且要炒得均匀,年糕才会入味。
Pudding cake itself have no flavor, other ingredients should be sufficient. Also, stir-fry evenly to make pudding cake tasty.

Stir-fried pudding cake with snow cabbage
雪菜炒年糕

20 分钟 Minutes 4 人 Persons

Tips

雪菜要用水加少许盐浸才浸出雪菜的咸味,大约浸30分钟。
Soak snow cabbage in salty water for 30 minutes to remove excess salty taste.

| 材料 | 水浸上海年糕6条 / 雪菜4棵 / 鸡汤2杯 / 蒜头2瓣 |
| 调味料 | 糖1茶匙 / 麻油1/2茶匙 / 老抽1/2茶匙 |

| Ingredients | 6 strips Shanghai pudding cake / 4 stalks snow cabbage / 2 cups chicken broth / 2 cloves garlic |
| Seasoning | 1 tsp sugar / 1/2 tsp sesame oil / 1/2 tsp dark soy sauce |

做法 Method

1. Drain Shanghai pudding cakes and slice.
2. Rinse snow cabbage, cut roots, drain, dice.
3. Peel garlic, rinse and chop.
4. Heat wok with 1/2 tbsp of oil, saute chopped garlic, add snow cabbage, Shanghai pudding cake, then add seasonings and chicken stock and cook until softened and soup dries up. Serve.

1. 上海年糕沥干水分，切片。
2. 雪菜洗净，切去根部，沥干水分，切末。
3. 蒜头去衣，洗净剁蓉。
4. 将锅烧热，下油约1/2汤匙，爆香蒜蓉，加入雪菜、上海年糕炒匀，再下调味料和鸡汤煮至上海年糕变软，而汤汁将收干即可盛起。

美食达人心动试味 / Gourmet's Comments

通菜炒好便要立即吃,放久了会变黑。
Serve immediately or water spinch will turns black quickly.

Stir-fried water spinach with flavored paste
惹味酱炒通菜

⏱ 10 分钟 / Minutes   👥 4 人 / Persons

Tips

炒通菜不要盖锅盖,否则菜会变黑。
Do not cover the lid when stir-frying water spinach, otherwise it will turns black.

材料	通菜500克 / 米酒2茶匙
配料	红辣椒1只 / 马拉盏（一种酱料）2汤匙 / 蒜蓉3茶匙 / XO酱3茶匙
调味料	糖1茶匙 / 鸡粉1茶匙

Ingredients	500 g water spinach / 2 tsps rice wine
Side Ingredient	1 red chilli / 2 tbsps Malaysian shrimp paste / 3 tsps chopped garlic / 3 tsps XO sauce
Seasoning	1 tsp sugar / 1 tsp chicken powder

做法

1. Rinse water spinach, remove old leaves, drain.
2. Rinse red chilli, seed, cut into shreds.
3. Heat the wok with 1/2 tbsp of oil, saute the side ingredients, add water spinach, drizzle wine, add seasonings, sprinkle with some water, mix well. Serve.

1. 通菜洗净，摘去老菜，沥干水分。
2. 红辣椒洗净，去籽，切丝。
3. 将锅烧热，下油约1/2汤匙，爆香配料，放入通菜，潵酒，加调味料，洒少许水，炒片刻即可上碟。

 蔬菜 Vegetables

美食达人心动试味 / Gourmet's Comments

浙醋不要加得太多，否则会夺去鸡蛋的味道。
Do not add too much vinegar, otherwise it will spoil the flavor of eggs.

Stir-fried artificial shark fin with egg whites
素翅炒蛋白

10 分钟 Minutes | 4 人 Persons

Tips

炒鸡蛋白要放较多油才会滑。
Add more oil when stir-frying egg whites.

| 材料 | 素翅60克 / 鸡蛋白4只 / 芥兰梗2棵 / 上汤6汤匙 |
| 调味料 | 盐1/2茶匙 / 姜汁1/3茶匙 / 胡椒粉1/4茶匙 / 姜丝4片 / 浙醋少许 |

| Ingredients | 60 g artificial shark fin / 4 egg whites / 2 stems broccoli / 6 tbsps soup |
| Seasoning | 1/2 tsp salt / 1/3 tsp ginger juice / 1/4 tsp pepper / 4 slices ginger(shredded) / vinegar |

做法 Method

1. Rinse artificial shark fin, bring a pot of water to a boil and blanch for a while, drain.

2. Beat egg whites into a large bowl, gently whisk, do not beat till bubbles form.

3. Rinse kale stems and dice.

4. Heat wok with 1/2 tbsp of oil, add artificial shark fin, broccoli stems and mix well, add seasonings and soup, mix well, dish up and set aside.

5. Heat the wok again with tbsp of oil, add egg whites and stir fry, return other ingredients to the wok, stir well and dish.

1. 素翅洗净，烧沸一锅水，加入素翅略烫片刻，沥干水分备用。

2. 鸡蛋白打入大碗中，轻轻搅匀，不要打至起泡。

3. 芥兰梗洗净，切粒备用。

4. 将锅烧热，下油约1/2汤匙，加入素翅、芥兰梗炒匀，下调味料和上汤炒匀，盛起备用。

5. 再将锅烧热，下油约1汤匙，加入鸡蛋白略炒，将其他材料回锅，炒匀上碟。

美食达人心动试味 / Gourmet's Comments

竹荪没有霉味。
Bamboo fungus must be blanched to removing musty flavor.

Stir-fried vegetables with bamboo fungus
素菜竹荪扒菜胆

15 分钟 Minutes — 4 人 Persons

Tips

竹荪一定要飞水才没有异味。
Bamboo fungus must blanched to remove unpleaant smell.

材料	上海白菜250克 / 竹荪20条 / 冬菇8只 / 蒜蓉1汤匙 姜3片 / 鸡汤3/4杯
调味料	盐1/2茶匙 / 糖1/4茶匙
芡汁	蚝油2茶匙 / 生粉1茶匙 / 水4汤匙

Ingredients	250 g Shanghai cabbage / 20 bamboo fungus / 8 dried black mushrooms / 1 tbsps chopped garlic / 3 slices ginger / 3/4 cup chicken broth
Seasoning	1/2 tsp salt / 1/4 tsp sugar
Sauce	2 tsps oyster Sauce / 1 tsp cornstarch / 4 tbsps water

做法 Method

1. Soak bamboo fungus, cut head and tail. Rinse dried black mushrooms, remove stalks. Blanch bamboo fungus and mushrooms, boil water and drain.

2. Rinse Shanghai cabbage, remove old leaves, cut into sections.

3. Heat the wok with 1/2 tbsp of oil, saute chopped garlic, add half of chicken broth, cook vegetables and dish up.

4. Heat the wok again with 1/2 tbsp of oil, saute ginger slices, add bamboo fungus and mushrooms and mix well, add the remaining chicken broth to cook for about 5 minutes. Cook until sauce is slightly thicken, dish up.

1. 竹荪浸软，剪去头尾。冬菇洗净，去蒂。把竹荪和冬菇飞水，沥干水分。

2. 上海白菜洗净，摘去老叶，切成菜胆备用。

3. 将锅烧热，下油约1/2汤匙，爆香蒜蓉，放入1/2份鸡汤，焯熟菜胆盛起备用。

4. 再将锅烧热，下油约1/2汤匙，爆香姜片，下竹荪和冬菇炒匀，加入余下鸡汤煮约5分钟。加上芡汁煮至汁稍浓，排放在菜胆上即可。

烹饪小词典
Cooking key words

常用调味品（附广东话发音）
Common seasonings

granulated sugar
砂糖 sa tong

brown sugar
黄糖 wong tong

slab sugar
片糖 pin tong

rock sugar
冰糖 bing tong

salt
盐 yim

corn oil
粟米油 sug mi yeo

olive oil
橄榄油 gem lam yeo

cooking oil
生油 seng yeo

butter
牛油 ngeo yeo

sesame oil
麻油 ma yeo

light soy sauce
生抽 seng chau

dark soy sauce
老抽 lou chau

oyster sauce
蚝油 hou yeo

fish sauce
鱼露 yu lou

ketchup
番茄酱 fan ke zeng

vinegar
醋 cou

wine
酒 zeo

cornstarch
鹰粟粉 ying sug fen

caltrop starch
生粉 seng fen

flour
面粉 min fen

MSG
味精 mei jing

chili bean sauce
豆瓣酱 deo ban zeng

satay sauce
沙爹酱 sa de zeng

miso
面酱 min zeng

fermented black beans
豆豉 deo xi

red beancurd
南乳 nam yu

fermented beancurd
腐乳 fu yu

black pepper sauce
黑椒烧汁 hak jiu xiu zeb

tabasco
辣椒汁 lad jiu zeb

curry powder
咖喱粉 ga lei fen

chicken powder
鸡粉 gei fen

chicken broth
鸡汤 gei tong

wasabi
芥辣 gai lad

pepper
胡椒粉 wu jiu fen

spices
香料 heng liu

honey
蜜糖 met tong

做菜和味道的常用语
Common phrases of cooking and tastes

普通话 Mandarin	英文 English	广东话 Cantonese（拼音）
食物味道 Taste		
熟	cooked	熟 sug
没熟	raw	未熟 mei sug
生 / 没熟	uncooked	生（未熟）seng
太咸	too salty	太咸 tai ham
太长时间	too long	太耐 tai noi
不够咸	not salty enough	唔够咸 em geo ham
不够甜	not sweet enough	唔够甜 em geo tim
香	aromatic	香 heng
臭	stink	臭 ceo
甜	sweet	甜 tim
酸	sour	酸 xun
苦	bitter	苦 fu
辣	spicy	辣 lad
咸	salty	咸 ham
煮菜方式 Cooking Method		
切片	slice	切片 qid pin
切长一点	cut longer	切长少少 qid ceng xiu-xiu
切短一点	cut shorter	切短少少 qid dün xiu-xiu
切块	cut into wedges	切块 qid fai
切粒	cut into dice	切粒粒 qid neb-neb
蒸	steam	蒸 jing
炸	deep-fry	炸 za
煎	shallow-fry	煎 jin
炒菜	stir-fry vegetables	炒菜 cao coi
焯菜	blanch vegetable	渌菜 lug coi
煲汤	cook soup	煲汤 bou tong
焖猪肉	stew pork	炆猪肉 men ju yug

常用技巧
Common skills

切角 Cut into triangles	把物料移动，切成三角形。 Roll the ingredient and cut into triangles.	
骨牌 Domino	物料先切成长形，再修切成长方形。 Cut the ingredient into long pieces, and then rectangles.	
滚刀块 Pieces in rolling knife	切成不规则的形状。 Cut ingredients into irregular shapes by rolling the ingredients.	
双飞 Butterflying	鱼肉切第一刀时不要切断，要余下少许，再切第二刀就要切断，两片鱼肉都要薄。 Do not cut off the fish at first knife to leave a little, then cut off at the second knife, two slices should be thin.	
去衣 Peel off the thin layer	把栗子放热水中煮1~2分钟，去掉栗子外皮。 Cook chestnuts into boiling water for 1-2 minutes, peel off the thin layer of chestnuts.	
去皮 Shave	用刨子削去物料外皮。 Shave off the skin of the ingredient.	
料头 Side ingredients	泛指姜、葱、蒜、干葱或辣椒，协助提升物料的香味。 Usually refer to ginger, spring onion, garlic, dried spring onion and chili which make ingredients more aromatic.	
泡油 Blanch with oil	将物料放入八成滚油中2~3分钟，取出沥油。 Cook ingredients in 80% boiled oil for 2-3 minutes, take out and drain.	
过冷河 Cooling off in water	食物放滚水中再捞起，放冻水中冲过，沥干水分。 Blanch ingredients. in boiling water and then dish up, put in cold water and drain.	
飞水（汆水） Blanch	物料放入滚水中焯2~3分钟，取出用冷水冲。 Cook ingredients in boiling water for 2-3 minutes, take out and rinse with cold water.	
白镬（锅） Wok without adding oil	没有添加任何物料、酱料或油等，只是把锅烧热后直接下物料烘干水分。 Without any ingredients, sauce or oil, dry the ingredients in a heated wok directly.	
回锅 Back to the wok	食物泡油后再放回锅中与其他材料一起炒。 Blanch food in boiling oil and then back into the wok and stir-fry along with other ingredients.	
爆香 Saute	用少量油加热，放入料头略煎至出味的程序。 Slightly shallow-fry seasonings till aromatic with some heated oil.	
埋芡 Thickening	食物煮熟后加生粉水。 Ingredients cooked and add cornstach solution to thicken.	

一餐中各种食物的摄取比例
The proportion of different food intake during a meal

2011年6月,美国农业部门(USDA)发表了一套新的健康饮食指南以取代有20年历史的膳食金字塔。这套新饮食指南以一个圆形餐碟做图示,被称作"我的餐碟"(My Plate)。餐碟被分成4份,分别代表4类食物,每餐中有一半是蔬菜及水果,当中蔬菜占较大部分;另外一半则是谷类及蛋白质,而谷类分量比蛋白质稍多。另外还建议一半以上的谷类为全谷物,并且因应年龄需要,每天还要加上1~2份乳制品。

相比传统膳食金字塔,"我的餐碟"更形象化,可提醒人们多吃蔬菜、水果。

蔬菜、水果之所以色泽鲜艳与其所含的植物营养素(Phytonutrients)有关,不同的颜色代表植物所含的营养素不同。像大家熟识的番茄红素、花青素等,都属于植物营养素,我们每餐应尽量选择不同种类的蔬菜、水果,以摄取多元化的植物营养素。

资料来源:chooseMyPlate.gov

看颜色食果蔬
Choose vegetables and fruit according to colour

颜色	植物营养素	例子	功效
红	番茄红素	番茄、红菜头、红辣椒、西瓜、西柚	• 降低患癌风险
红	花青素	红葡萄、红洋葱、草莓、小红莓、山莓	• 抗氧化及消炎,有助消除体内自由基及发炎因子,活化脑细胞 • 保护心脏
橙/黄	α胡萝卜素、β胡萝卜素	番茄、南瓜、胡萝卜、黄辣椒、木瓜、橘子、杏子、柿子	• 保护视力 • 提升免疫力 • 降低患癌及心脏病风险 • 保持黏膜健康
橙/黄	玉米黄素	玉米(粟米)、橘、水蜜桃	• 抗氧化,预防黄斑区受自由基侵害,维护视力健康
橙/黄	维生素C	柠檬、橙、菠萝	• 提升免疫力
橙/黄	叶酸	橙、哈密瓜、芒果	• 负责制造红细胞,预防贫血
绿	叶黄素、玉米黄素	绿豆、芦笋、青椒、菠菜、芥蓝、西兰花、生菜、猕猴桃	• 抗氧化,预防黄斑区受自由基及日光伤害,保护视力 • 降低患癌及心脏病风险
绿	靛基质、异硫氰酸酯	西兰花、椰菜	• 降低患癌风险
绿	有机硫化合物(如蒜辣素)	青葱、韭菜	• 降低患癌风险 • 保护心脏
绿	叶酸	所有绿叶蔬菜,如菠菜、芥蓝等	• 负责制造红细胞,预防贫血
蓝/紫	花青素	茄子、蓝莓、黑莓、紫色葡萄、梅子、无花果	• 抗氧化及消炎,有助消除体内自由基及发炎因子,活化脑细胞 • 保护心脏
白	有机硫化合物(如蒜辣素)	洋葱、蒜头、姜、白萝卜、蘑菇	• 降低患癌风险 • 保护心脏
白	钾质	香蕉、马铃薯	• 稳定血压